This Book Belongs to...

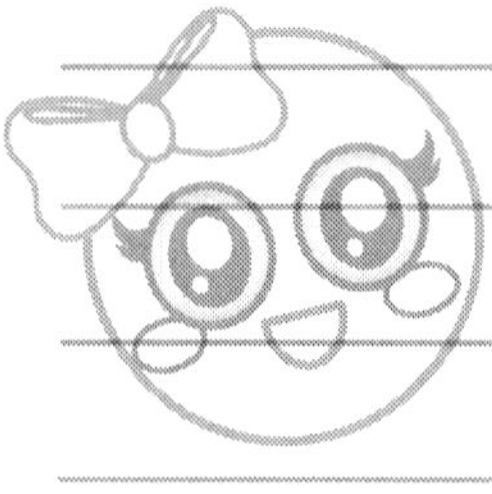

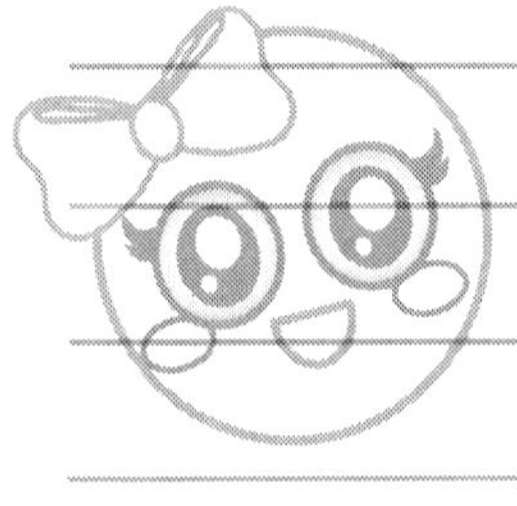

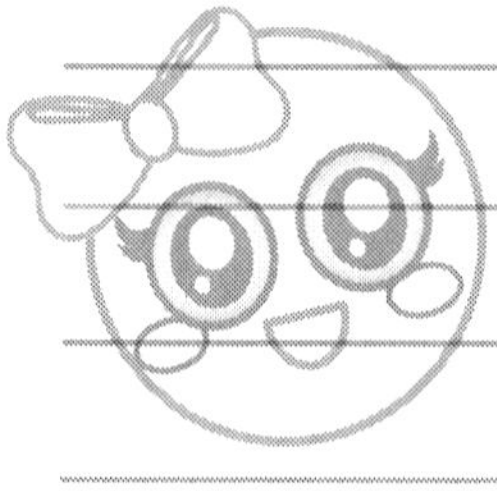

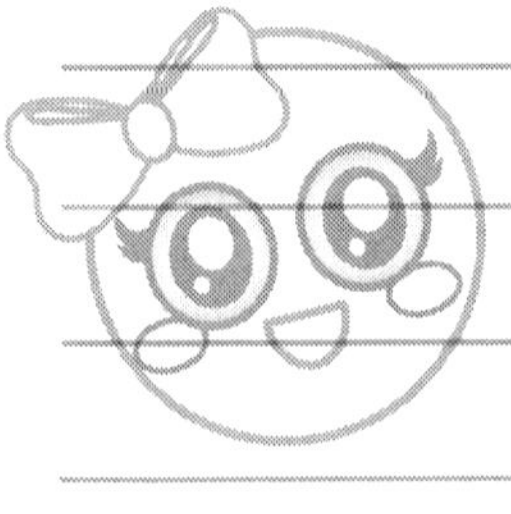

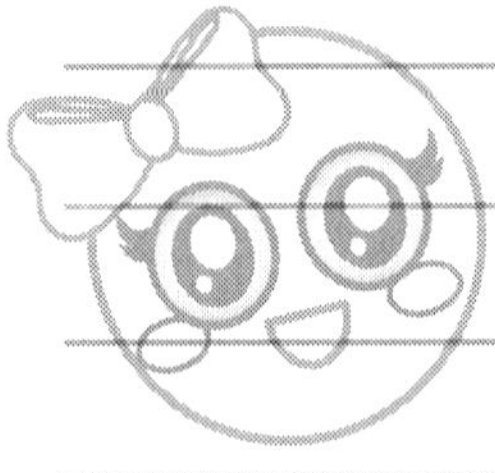

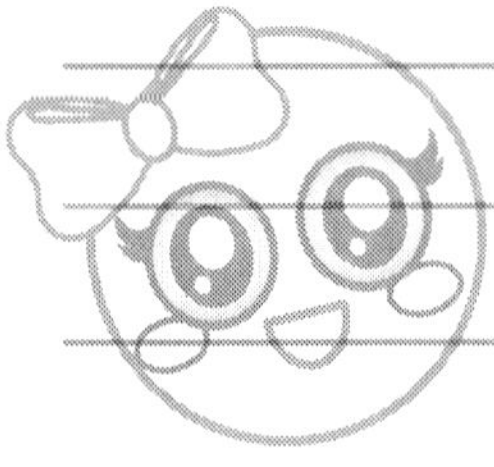

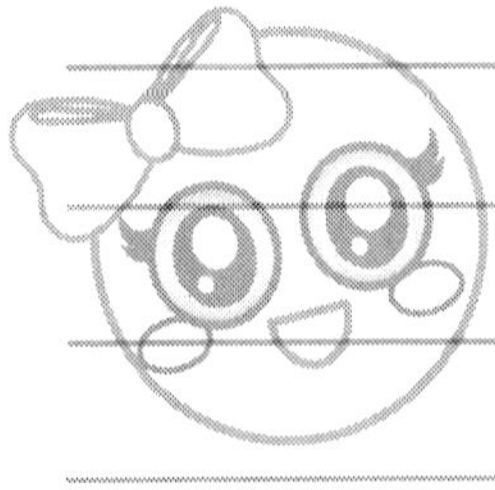

70646081R00069

Made in the USA
San Bernardino, CA
04 March 2018